The Giver

Lightbox Literature Studies

Tammy Gagne

LIGHTB◆X
openlightbox.com

LIGHTBOX

Go to
www.openlightbox.com
and enter this book's
unique code.

ACCESS CODE

L B P 6 7 4 5 6

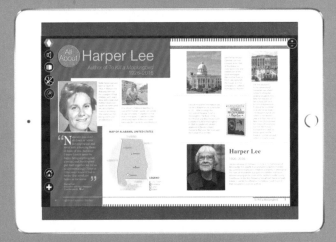

Lightbox is an all-inclusive digital solution for the teaching and learning of curriculum topics in an original, groundbreaking way. Lightbox is based on National Curriculum Standards.

STANDARD FEATURES OF LIGHTBOX

 AUDIO High-quality narration using text-to-speech system

 WEBLINKS Curated links to external, child-safe resources

 INTERACTIVE MAPS Interactive maps and aerial satellite imagery

 VIDEOS Embedded high-definition video clips

 SLIDESHOWS Pictorial overviews of key concepts

 QUIZZES Ten multiple choice questions that are automatically graded and emailed for teacher assessment

 ACTIVITIES Printable PDFs that can be emailed and graded

 TRANSPARENCIES Step-by-step layering of maps, diagrams, charts, and timelines

 KEY WORDS Matching key concepts to their definitions

 MORE Extra information and details on the subject

 FIRST HAND Letters, diaries, and other primary sources

 DOCS Speeches, newspaper articles, and other historical documents

Contents

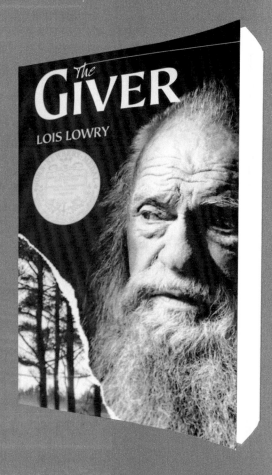

2   Access Lightbox Student Edition

4   All About Lois Lowry

6   Setting of the Novel

8   Time Period of the Novel

10   Conflict in the Novel

12   Introducing the Characters

14   The Art of Storytelling

16   Theme in the Novel

18   Symbolism in the Novel

20   The Use of Language

22   Impact of the Novel at the Time of Publishing

24   Impact of the Novel Now

26   Perspectives on Freedom of Expression

28   Writing a Comparative Essay

30   Key Words/Literary Terms

31   Index

32   Log on to www.openlightbox.com

EXTENSION ACTIVITY

Conducting an Interview

Students will conduct an interview with a community member about a time period in their community's history, and submit an audio recording and transcript of the interview. An exemplary interview will meet the following criteria.

- Clearly defines the purpose of the interview
- Conducts thorough background research to inform the focus of the interview and the questions
- Drafts a complete list of thoughtful, in-depth, and varied questions prior to the interview
- Interviews a subject with relevant knowledge on the topic and time period in question
- Asks questions in a logical order, building upon each other
- Treats the interview subject in a polite, respectful, and professional manner
- Does not interrupt or rush the interview subject
- Shows interest and enthusiasm in responses and follow-up questions
- Chooses follow-up questions that demonstrate active listening
- Asks for clarification and further details when necessary
- Asks questions about personal experiences related to the topic
- Asks questions regarding factual information and the interview subject's opinion on the topic
- Asks creative questions that reflect fresh insights on the topic
- Records the full interview in a quiet environment
- Organizes and edits the interview transcript to be clear and factual

All About Lois Lowry

Author of *The Giver*
1937–

Lois Ann Hammersberg was born on March 20, 1937, in Honolulu, Hawai'i, the second child of Robert and Katharine Hammersberg. She would not remain there long, though, as her father was a dentist in the United States Army and their family moved often because of his career. While her father was stationed overseas during World War II, Lois moved to Pennsylvania with her mother and older sister. There, they lived with her grandfather, who spent time reading books with Lois in his vast library.

> **❝I** tried in writing it [*The Giver*] to make it seductive so that for the first third of the book, I hope, readers will feel as though this is a good place to live. There's no crime. There's no inequality. There's no discrimination. And then gradually . . . you become aware, in an uncomfortable way, that maybe it isn't such a great place.**❞**
>
> Lois Lowry
> *Reading Rockets* interview, 2009

MAP OF NEW ENGLAND, UNITED STATES

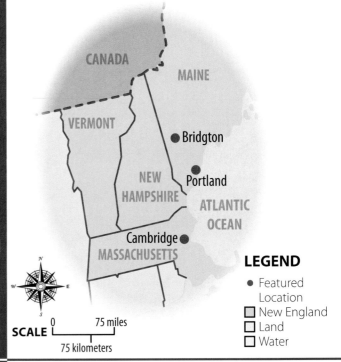

CANADA
MAINE
VERMONT
NEW HAMPSHIRE
• Bridgton
• Portland
ATLANTIC OCEAN
Cambridge •
MASSACHUSETTS

SCALE
0   75 miles
75 kilometers

LEGEND
- • Featured Location
- ☐ New England
- ☐ Land
- ☐ Water

Lois married Donald Lowry and moved with him to New England in 1956. She graduated from the University of Southern Maine in 1972. While pursuing her master's degree, Lois worked as a freelance journalist, writing stories and articles for magazines and newspapers. In 1977, the couple divorced.

The Giver, a tale of a futuristic totalitarian society, was published in 1993. At the time, it was considered groundbreaking. It remains Lowry's most successful published work to date. The **dystopian** novel has won numerous awards and sold millions of copies. The story has also been adapted into a play, a feature film, and even an opera.

Lois published her first novel, *A Summer to Die*, in 1977. Partly autobiographical, the book told the story of a young girl whose sister was dying of leukemia. Like the main character, Lois had lost her own sister to cancer. Although she had lost her sister as an adult, she based the opening scene of the book on a memory from their childhood.

TEACHER NOTES

🗺 **Google Maps**

University of Southern Maine, Bedford Street, Portland, Maine
Explore the campus of the University of Southern Maine, where Lowry got her degree.

🌐 **Weblink**

As Easy as ABC
Examine Jim Pollard's article in *The Observer* discussing writing as a form of self-directed therapy.

1. Compare and contrast the benefits and drawbacks of talking therapy and therapeutic writing. How are the reasons Pollard gives for choosing therapeutic writing over talking therapy valid? Which form of therapy would you choose to engage in? Why?
2. How might therapeutic writing affect an author's works? In what ways might therapeutic writing produce better material?

Today, Lois splits her time between her Cambridge, Massachusetts home and a farmhouse in Bridgton, Maine. She maintains a strict schedule, dedicated to writing for at least five hours each day. She also regularly writes a blog on her website. Lois's spare time is spent reading, gardening, traveling, and being with her two children and six grandchildren. She also enjoys going to the movies whenever she can. To date, her collected works total more than 40 books for children and young adults.

Analyzing a Video

Students will watch and assess a video related to a component of the novel, and write an analysis of the video. An exemplary video analysis will meet the following criteria.

- Identifies the purpose of the video
- Identifies the intended audience of the video
- Describes how the content of the video is presented
- Summarizes the information and opinions presented in the video
- Analyzes the quality of the content presented in the video
- Assesses the effectiveness of the video
- Discusses the technical aspects of the video and whether or not these enhance the content
- Determines whether the images and graphics used in the video relate to the content
- Determines whether the video is easy to follow and understand
- Gives the analysis a clear and consistent purpose
- Organizes the analysis in a logical, effective manner
- Presents a strong, clear argument about the video
- Provides strong and accurate details to support the argument about the video
- Considers other perspectives on the purpose and effectiveness of the video
- Makes connections between the video and the novel
- Properly integrates quotations from the video
- Cites all sources used in the analysis

Setting of the Novel

*T*he *Giver* takes place in an obscure yet intensely orderly community. Lowry never divulges the location of the community, but she does show the reader that it is a place with many rules, which the inhabitants must obey without question. Instead of offering details about geography, Lowry sets the opening scenes carefully through language and feelings. A sense of order dominates the community from the first page. People live in dwellings that are all the same. It is also established that other communities just like this one are nearby.

The setting is one of precision. The community's rules are far more important than its location. As the book begins, the protagonist, Jonas, recalls a pilot who was "released" from their community after what appeared to be a simple mistake. Although it is not yet clear what this means, both the community members and the reader understand it is a serious punishment.

Snapshot

Origins of Dystopia

The word *dystopia* is derived from late-eighteenth century Greek words, with *dis* meaning "bad" and *topos* meaning "place."

Popular dystopian novels include *Brave New World* by Aldous Huxley (1932), *Nineteen Eighty-Four* by George Orwell (1949), and *The Handmaid's Tale* by Margaret Atwood (1985).

In early 2017, readers showed a renewed interest in dystopian fiction. During the last week of January, sales of Orwell's *Nineteen Eighty-Four* increased by 9,500 percent.

Strict Obedience

"Next, Mother, who held a prominent position at the Department of Justice, talked about her feelings. Today a repeat offender had been brought before her, someone who had broken the rules before. Someone who she hoped had been adequately and fairly punished, and who had been restored to his place: to his job, his home, his family unit. To see him brought before her a second time caused her overwhelming feelings of frustration and anger. And even guilt, that she hadn't made a difference in his life. 'I feel frightened for him, too,' she confessed. 'You know that there's no third chance. The rules say that if there's a third **transgression**, he simply has to be released. Jonas shivered. He knew it happened. There was even a boy in his group of Elevens whose father had been released years before. No one ever mentioned it; the disgrace was unspeakable. It was hard to imagine."

Chapter 1

The predictability and safety of the community in *The Giver* is based on Lowry's feelings about her childhood home in Tokyo, Japan. Despite living in a foreign country, the community in which Lowry lived with her family was largely Americanized. The culture, the language, and the architecture were familiar to her. When she rode her bicycle to a nearby neighborhood, though, she would immediately notice the startling differences between the two communities. Although this area was adjacent to her Japanese home, people dressed and acted quite differently, which made Lowry feel like an outsider. She used these childhood experiences to construct the fictitious Elsewhere, a place the novel's characters perceive as dangerous due to its differences.

The 2014 film version of *The Giver* illustrated the community presented in the novel through black and white cinematography. The movie characters wore matching clothes and rode identical bicycles. Even their homes were the same. This choice by the filmmakers had the effect of stripping the characters of their uniqueness and individuality, contributing to the tone of the setting as established in the novel.

TEACHER NOTES

▶ **Video**

Film Clip of *The Giver* Opera
Analyze the setting created in the operatic adaptation of *The Giver*.

1. Which elements of the set design and costuming are most effective in the portrayal of the *The Giver*'s setting, as it appears in the novel? Which elements of the set design and costuming feel inconsistent or ineffective? Provide reasons for your opinions.
2. Is the operatic adaptation consistent with the tone generated by the setting in the novel? Why or why not?

🌐 **Weblink**

13 Pros and Cons of Conformity in Society
Examine this post discussing the benefits and drawbacks of conformity in society.

1. What might be the end result of a society with no conformity? Are there any scenarios in which anarchy could be a viable way for societies to live? How could peaceful anarchy exist?
2. In what ways is conformity dangerous? What is the end result of a society that never questions its rules, laws, or leaders?

Analyzing Bias in a Document

Students will analyze the bias that exists in a document from a different historical time and place, and how that bias shapes the opinions presented in the document. An exemplary analysis of bias in a document will meet the following criteria.

- Identifies the main points presented in the document
- Offers an in-depth interpretation of the document
- Differentiates between facts and opinions
- Identifies the writer
- Presents information about the writer
- Assesses the writer's reliability
- Determines the goals for the document
- Considers and assesses the writer's perspective
- Determines the writer's intended audience
- Identifies when and where the document was written
- Describes the historical context for the time and place in which the document was created, and analyzes how this context might have shaped the opinions expressed in the document
- Infers political or societal influences that may have shaped the opinions presented in the document
- Determines whether the writer had first-hand knowledge of the topic or event, or whether they are reporting as a secondary source
- Determines the document's bias
- Infers what interests the writer might have had that led them to create this document
- Explores other sources related to the topic of the document

Time Period of the Novel

The Giver is set at some point in the future. Although Lowry does not provide an exact date, the month of December looms near as the story begins. Eleven-year-old Jonas is feeling anxious about a ceremony that will be held in December. At this ceremony, the focus will be on him and the rest of the youth in the community.

Waiting for December

"He had waited a long time for this special December. Now that it was almost upon him, he wasn't frightened, but he was . . . eager, he decided. He was eager for it to come. And he was excited, certainly. All of the Elevens were excited about the event that would be coming so soon. But there was a little shudder of nervousness when he thought about it, about what might happen. Apprehensive, Jonas decided. That's what I am."

Chapter 1

The Giver Explains the Sameness

"Our people made that choice, the choice to go to Sameness. Before my time, before the previous time, back and back and back. We relinquished color when we relinquished sunshine and did away with difference. We gained control of many things. But we had to let go of others."

Chapter 12

Time in *The Giver* is represented by the characters' ages and their related responsibilities. Jonas is referred to as an Eleven, while his sister, Lily, is a Seven. At first these terms seem similar to those used in the real world, but it soon becomes apparent that being an Eleven is not like being a sixth-grader. Something significant is about to happen in Jonas's life as he moves on to become a Twelve.

Lowry's father suffered from severe memory loss in his senior years. His inability to remember was one of the things that inspired Lowry to write a novel about memories. When Lois showed her father a picture of her late sister, Helen, he asked what had happened to her. After having to explain that she had died, Lois wondered if it would be easier for people not to have memories at all. *The Giver* was born from her wish that people did not have to carry around painful memories.

The first drug to treat Alzheimer's disease was approved by the Federal Drug Administration (FDA) in 1993, the same year that Lowry published *The Giver*. A year later, former U.S. President Ronald Reagan announced that he was suffering from the memory-destroying illness. In an interview with *People* magazine in 2017, his former executive assistant Peggy Grande, described Reagan's revelation to the American people as something he did "frankly, forthrightly and with optimism."

TEACHER NOTES

👁 First Hand

What if You Could Control Memory: Writing *The Giver*
Analyze the lecture given by Lois Lowry on the process of writing *The Giver*.

1. In her lecture, Lowry cites the passage "I can see that it was a dangerous way to live." How might having memories be a dangerous way to live? What kind of memories could be considered particularly dangerous?
2. Analyze the symbolism of fire from the passages read by Lowry. How effective is fire as a symbol for memory or memories? Which other imagery in the novel would be an appropriate comparison to the nature of memory?

📄 Document

FDA Approves First Alzheimer's Disease Treatment Medication
Analyze the 1993 article from *Los Angeles Times* writer Marlene Cimons discussing the release of Tacrine.

1. Prescription drugs such as Tacrine often come with as many side effects as they do benefits. Are the side effects of a drug worth a "small but meaningful benefit" of taking a drug? Why or why not?
2. Cimons states in her article that medical experts believe that instances of Alzheimer's are under-reported. Why might this be? How could this problem be mitigated or solved?

Writing a Short Story

Students will choose an excerpt from the novel and use it as their inspiration in writing a short story. An exemplary short story will meet the following criteria.

- Engages the reader from the opening line
- Establishes a clear, consistent point of view
- Introduces a narrator and a setting
- Develops an engaging conflict at the heart of the narrative to build tension and keep the reader interested
- Develops characters and events through purposeful and well-crafted literary devices
- Creates a logical progression of events in the narrative that build upon each other using various techniques
- Explores ideas, concepts, and writing styles with creativity and originality
- Demonstrates a high level of skill in using appropriate narrative techniques to tell the story
- Concludes the narrative in a thoughtful, effective manner appropriate to the narrative
- Uses varied, purposeful diction and syntax to affect style and serve the narrative
- Writes with clarity, imagination, and a unique, personal voice
- Does not use stereotypes or clichés
- Uses effective, believable dialogue
- Uses correct spelling, grammar, and punctuation

Conflict in the Novel

Conflict is what keeps a story engaging. The struggle between the main character, or the protagonist, and opposing forces creates challenges that must be resolved by the story's end. Often the protagonist's biggest struggle is with another person, the antagonist, but conflict can also come from other forces. Many novels include more than one type of conflict.

The Four Major Types of Conflict in Literature

MAN vs. MAN

MAN vs. SELF

The Lion, The Witch and the Wardrobe by C.S. Lewis features four children who discover a magical land called Narnia. There, they make an enemy of a malicious White Witch, who fears a prophecy that her reign over Narnia will end at the hand of four humans. After one of their party, Edmund, is taken by the witch, the children befriend a powerful lion named Aslan, who promises to help them save Edmund.

Sometimes a character's most serious conflict is internal. In the novel *Holes* by Louis Sachar, the protagonist, Stanley, is sent to a boys' work camp as punishment for a crime he did not commit. The camp is a horrible place with a vicious warden, who mistreats the boys. In order to change his future, Stanley must believe in himself and champion the cause of the abused.

MAN vs. SOCIETY

MAN vs. NATURE

Sometimes a protagonist struggles with society. In the *Divergent* series by Veronica Roth, the main character, Tris, fights against the structure of her society. In this futuristic story, people are divided into factions based on their skills. When Tris is identified as divergent, she rebels against the idea that people must choose to be just one thing. She rallies many other characters to join her fight against society.

In many adventure stories, the conflict is between the main character and nature. A protagonist might struggle in an intense storm, become lost, or be hunted by a wild animal. The main character in Daniel Defoe's *Robinson Crusoe* is faced with all three of these struggles. After being shipwrecked on a tropical island, Crusoe realizes he is the lone survivor. In this man-versus-nature conflict, the island is the antagonist.

Types of Conflict in *The Giver*

The two main types of conflict in *The Giver* are man versus society and man versus man. Both of these conflicts propel the story forward.

Man versus Society

"'Jonas,' the Giver said after a moment, 'It is true that it has been this way for what seems like forever. But the memories tell us that it has not always been. People felt things once. You and I have been part of that, so we know. We know that they once felt things like pride, like sorrow, and—'
        'And love,' Jonas added."

Chapter 20

Jonas   The Giver   Society

Man versus Man

"'Don't play it anymore,' Jonas pleaded.
'I'm the one who's training for Assistant Recreation Director,' Asher pointed out angrily.
Games aren't your area of expertness.'
        'Expertise,' Jonas corrected him automatically.
        'Whatever. You can't say what we play, even if you are going to be the new Receiver.'"

Chapter 17

Jonas   Asher

 More

The Types of Conflict in *The Giver*

Analyze the citations from the novel revealing the types of conflict as they appear in *The Giver.*

1. How do these excerpts of conflict reveal the novel's theme? Explain and defend your ideas.
2. Analyze Lowry's development of conflict between Jonas and Asher. How does their conflict deepen or reveal character? How does it drive the story's plot and themes?

Weblink

Literature Is Not A Conflict-Free Zone

Examine the excerpt from Jonathan Gottschall's book *The Storytelling Animal: How Stories Make Us Human*.

1. What merit is there to Gotschall's claims about the power of story to train, prepare, and help people work through real-life issues? Provide evidence for your ideas.
2. People write their own stories each day with the places they go, the people they meet, the things that they say, and the choices they make. Is it possible to live a life story that is free of conflict? What might be the end result of a life lived in this way?

Introducing the Characters

Characterization is how writers introduce the characters to the reader. This can happen in several ways. A character's name or age may be told directly to the reader in the narrative. Other writers enhance their stories by revealing character details and traits through what characters say and do. Much can be learned about characters by observing their actions and dialogue.

Most of the characterization of *The Giver* takes place in the beginning of the book. The reader is introduced to Jonas on the first page, as he experiences the memory of the unfortunate pilot who flew over the community without permission. Lowry compares Jonas's feeling of fear to his distress over the upcoming Ceremony of Twelves.

Major Characters in *The Giver*

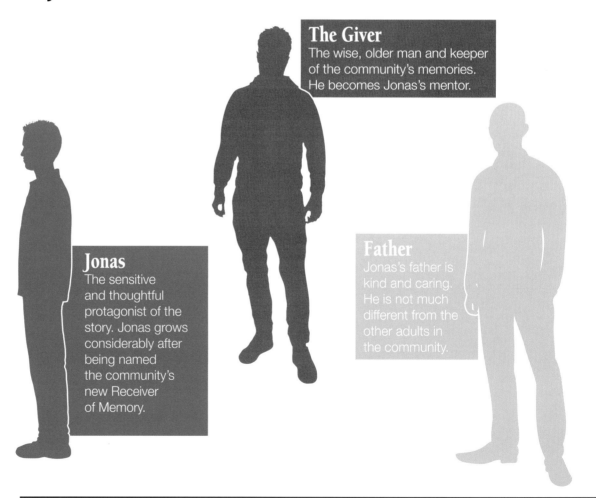

The Giver
The wise, older man and keeper of the community's memories. He becomes Jonas's mentor.

Jonas
The sensitive and thoughtful protagonist of the story. Jonas grows considerably after being named the community's new Receiver of Memory.

Father
Jonas's father is kind and caring. He is not much different from the other adults in the community.

Dynamic characters change as the story moves forward, often as a result of conflicts. Jonas, for instance, is respectful of the community's rules, but inwardly, he questions whether he should follow them. He eventually comes to believe that sometimes people need to break rules to do what is right.

Although static characters do not change, they still serve an important purpose in driving stories forward. Jonas's father is a shy and quiet person who works as a Nurturer. Part of his job is releasing weak or sick infants from the community. Jonas is greatly bothered when he learns this.

Round characters reveal many details about themselves through the course of the narrative. Both Jonas and the Giver fall into this category. Flat characters also help drive the storyline but in a smaller way. They display a single personality trait or none at all. In *The Giver*, a couple who lost their first child when he fell into the river is given a replacement child at the December Ceremony. His name, like the little boy who died, is Caleb. Both these boys and their parents are flat characters, as they show the reader more about the community, but nothing else happens to them.

Lily
Jonas's talkative younger sister. At the beginning of the story, she is becoming an Eight.

Fiona
Jonas's other good friend. She is given the job of Nurturer, but understands little about the true, ominous nature of her work.

Mother
Jonas's mother works for the Department of Justice and has an unquestioning belief in the importance of the community's rules.

Asher
Jonas's best friend is a friendly boy who loves playing games. He is the community's Assistant Director of Recreation.

◉ More
Character Development in *The Giver*
Analyze the characters in *The Giver* using the descriptions on the character map and excerpts from each character. Then, choose a character and answer the following questions.

1. Which of the writer's techniques are most effective at revealing this character's traits? Why?
2. In what ways is the characterization of this character ineffective? What could be done to improve this character's function in the novel? Defend your ideas with evidence.

🌐 Weblink
The Secret to Crafting Genuine Characters for Your Novel
Assess the blog post discussing elements of characterization.

1. Why do the characters in *The Giver* seem largely absent of behavioral or personality tics? How would the story benefit from addition of these details?
2. How would giving characters "word whiskers" in *The Giver* have detracted from its tone? How might it have improved the characterization? What reasons might authors have for omitting these details?

Creating a Literary Device Analysis Booklet

Students will analyze the author's use of a literary device in the novel, and create a booklet to present this analysis. An exemplary literary device analysis booklet will meet the following criteria.

- Defines the chosen literary device accurately and in detail
- Places the definition of the literary device at the beginning of the booklet
- Provides strong, specific examples of how this literary device is used in the novel
- Describes examples in detail, with quotations properly integrated
- Includes thorough analysis of the use, purpose, and effectiveness of each example of how the chosen literary device is used in the novel
- Arranges all pages logically
- Examples are organized chronologically
- Provides no more than one example and its analysis per page
- Creates a neat, well-organized, and attractive booklet
- Booklet is colorful and displays the student's creativity
- Uses illustrations to represent the chosen literary device and the examples of how it is used in the novel

The Art of Storytelling

Storytelling is a way to entertain, engage with others, teach, or communicate perspectives on society. When writing his or her story, the writer structures the narrative in a particular way. A narrative, or story, is a series of events that is often logically arranged. The writer uses different types of literary devices to create a distinct style and convey the narrative's overall message. In order to tell her story effectively, Lois Lowry structured her narrative, created a plot, and used a number of literary devices in *The Giver*.

Structure of a Narrative

Each narrative has a structure that writers keep in mind when creating a story. The most common narrative structure, known as dramatic structure or Freytag's Pyramid, consists of five main components, which are all used in *The Giver*.

Freytag's Pyramid

② Rising Action
The events that create increased drama or tension.

③ Climax
The moment of greatest tension in the story's action, when the protagonist faces his or her conflict.

④ Falling Action
The events that take place after the climax, leading to the end of the story.

① Exposition
The beginning of the story, where the characters and setting are introduced.

⑤ Resolution
The end of the story, when the conflicts are resolved and the action comes to a conclusion.

Plot

Every novel has a plot, or events that move the story from one point to the next. The series in which these events take place is called the plotline. A well-organized plotline helps the narrative flow smoothly.

Plot Points in Chapter 20 of *The Giver*

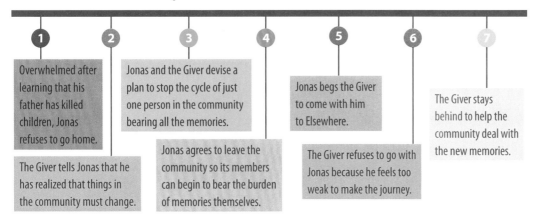

1. Overwhelmed after learning that his father has killed children, Jonas refuses to go home.

The Giver tells Jonas that he has realized that things in the community must change.

2. Jonas and the Giver devise a plan to stop the cycle of just one person in the community bearing all the memories.

3. Jonas agrees to leave the community so its members can begin to bear the burden of memories themselves.

4. Jonas begs the Giver to come with him to Elsewhere.

5. The Giver refuses to go with Jonas because he feels too weak to make the journey.

6. The Giver stays behind to help the community deal with the new memories.

7.

Literary Devices

The tools a writer uses to tell a story are called literary devices. While there are many literary devices, the two main types are literary elements and literary techniques. Literary elements help make novels interesting. Most literary elements exist in every story. Literary techniques, however, vary depending on the writer's style and effect he or she wishes to achieve.

Literary Elements
A literary element is a feature of a narrative that appears in almost every work of literature. The narrative needs these major features in order to be effective and engaging.

Action
What happens in the story.

Narrative Point of View
The perspective from which a story is told.

Moral
A lesson that the reader learns from the story.

Literary Techniques
Literary techniques are the various ways a writer can manipulate language to convey meaning or to create a distinct style.

Metaphor
A word or phrase is used as a symbol or figure of speech for the sake of effect.

Rhetorical Question
Rhetorical questions do not need answers, but they prompt the reader to think about them. They give insight into what a character is thinking.

Simile
Describes one thing by comparing it to another.

▶ Video

The Final Scenes of *The Giver*
Examine the final scenes of the book as they are depicted in the 2014 film adaptation of *The Giver*.

1. Think about the flashes of video that play after Jonas crosses the border to Elsewhere. What is the intended effect of these images on the audience by the filmmaker? Why do you think these images were chosen?
2. Compare and contrast the ending of the novel with how it is depicted in the final moments of the film. How different or similar is the content? Which of the two mediums delivers the intended message of the novel's final scenes more effectively? Provide solid reasoning for your opinions.

More

Examples of Literary Techniques from the Novel
Analyze the author's use of literary techniques and how they contribute to the narrative of *The Giver*.

1. Choose one literary technique used in the novel. In what particular way did the author use this literary technique? How effective was its usage?
2. What arguments can be made for the use of your chosen literary technique in a text? If this technique were overused or underutilized, what effect might it have on an author's work?

Students will complete a thorough research process to prepare for a writing assignment, and organize their research in a logical manner that supports their writing. An exemplary research process will meet the following criteria.

- Creates a goal for the research, based on the topic and working thesis
- Creates specific, thoughtful, and inventive research questions that are relevant to the topic of the writing assignment
- Produces a list of categories, key words, and related ideas to effectively assist in researching
- Uses high-quality sources that pertain to the topic and come in a variety of formats, such as books, journals, primary sources, websites, and databases
- Determines accuracy of all sources
- Uses sources that provide balanced research and various perspectives on the topic in question
- Takes notes to highlight the key facts and ideas in order to answer all research questions
- Extracts relevant, detailed information from the sources during the note-taking process
- Organizes the research notes in a clear and concise manner
- Organizes the research notes logically and in a way that sets up the information and ideas for analysis and the writing process
- Analyzes the information and produces ideas and points to support the working thesis
- Uses an effective and suitable format to present all research
- Properly cites all sources used

Theme in the Novel

The theme of a novel is its underlying topic, or main idea. Themes can be evident or difficult to identify and understand. Many novels have multiple themes, although one theme may be stronger than another. It is important to not mistake the subject of a story for its theme. Novels about completely different subjects can have a common theme.

Values

It is impossible to identify a novel's themes without considering the characters' values. Values, or beliefs, are what drives the characters' behavior. Readers gain a sense of the characters' values through their words, thoughts, and actions. Values often play a large role in the story's conflict. Characters with differing values juxtapose one another and help to reveal the theme of the novel. Characters with evolving values can also help to highlight aspects of a novel's theme.

Major Themes of *The Giver*

The dangers of **conformity**, the value of individuality, and the importance of memories are all major themes in *The Giver*. This novel shows the reader that when taken to extremes, sameness can lead to empty, meaningless lives. In an effort to create a **utopian** society, the community has actually built a dystopian society.

Jonas

The Dangers of Conformity

"Jonas stared at the screen, waiting for something to happen. But nothing did. The little twin lay motionless. His father was putting things away. Folding the blanket. Closing the cupboard.

Once again, as he had on the playing field, he felt the choking sensation. Once again, he saw the face of the light-haired, bloodied soldier as life left his eyes. The memory came back.

He killed it! My father killed it! Jonas said to himself, stunned at what he was realizing. He continued to stare at the screen numbly."

Chapter 19

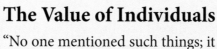

The Value of Individuals

"No one mentioned such things; it was not a rule, but was considered rude to call attention to things that were unsettling or different about individuals."

Chapter 3

Importance of Memories

"'The worst part of holding the memories is not the pain. It's the loneliness of it. Memories need to be shared.'

'I've started to share them with you,' Jonas said, trying to cheer him.

'That's true. And having you here with me over the past year has made me realize that things must change. For years I've felt that they should, but it seemed so hopeless.'

'Now for the first time, I think there might be a way,' the Giver said slowly. 'And you brought it to my attention, barely'—he glanced at the clock—'two hours ago.'

Jonas watched him, and listened."

Chapter 20

Jonas

Secondary Themes

Other themes in *The Giver* include family, friendship, and love. As heads of the family unit, parents keep their children fed, clean, and safe. They care for them, but only according to the rules. Superficial friendships are an acceptable part of life in the community, but none of these relationships include emotions. Love is a word that is no longer used or even understood. Lowry conveys the theme of love by showing the reader how bleak life would be without it.

 Weblink

The Forgetting Pill Erases Painful Memories Forever
Examine the article in *Wired* discussing memory modification.

1. What ethical concerns are inherent in the modification of memory? When might the benefits of memory modification outweigh its risks?
2. What risks and dangers are involved in being able to modify or erase any memory at any time? How might such a technology be abused?

 More

Major and Secondary Themes
Analyze the author's development of themes over the course of the novel.

1. Choose a secondary theme from this spread and analyze its appearances in the novel. How does this theme first emerge? Which is the most poignant example of this theme in the novel? Provide reasons for your position.
2. What particular commentary might the author be making about life as a result of this theme's presence in the text? Explain and defend your ideas.
3. Choose a major theme presented on pages 16–17. In what ways does your chosen secondary theme relate to this major theme? Does it deepen or detract from the major theme? How or in what way?

Creating a
Symbolism Poster

Students will choose one of the
other symbols listed on page 19
and analyze its role in the novel.
They will then create a poster
to present their analysis. An
exemplary symbolism poster will
meet the following criteria.

- Presents a clear purpose that is
  conveyed throughout the poster
- Shows an understanding of the
  concept of symbolism and the role
  it plays in the novel
- Provides an in-depth analysis of
  what the symbol represents
- Discusses the role the symbol plays
  in the novel
- Clearly indicates where the symbol
  appears in the novel
- Uses specific, detailed examples
  from the text to support
  the analysis
- Makes clear connections to the text
- Properly integrates all quotations
- Organizes the information in a
  logical, easy-to-read manner
- Includes high-quality graphics that
  relate to the symbol and effectively
  enhance understanding of the topic
- Features clear and concise writing
- Uses correct spelling, grammar,
  and punctuation
- Clearly labels items of importance
- Headings and subheadings are
  clear and easy to read
- Uses layout to creatively enhances
  the information
- Creates a poster that is attractive in
  terms of layout, design,
  and organization
- Shows a strong effort by
  the student

Symbolism in the Novel

Symbolism is a literary technique that helps the reader understand the themes of the story. Often a symbol is a tangible object, something that can be seen and touched. Words and concepts can also serve as symbols. Readers can gain a deeper understanding of stories and their meanings by identifying and analyzing the writer's use of symbols. Some symbols are intended to reveal a writer's feelings about specific ideas or concepts. Symbolism can help give a story's events, characters, and themes an interconnected, universal feel.

The Sled

"Sled, he knew abruptly. He was sitting on a thing called a sled. And the sled itself seemed to be poised at the top of a long, extended mound that rose from the very land where he was. Even as he thought the word "mound," his new consciousness told him hill.

Then the sled, with Jonas himself upon it, began to move through the snowfall, and he understood instantly that now he was going downhill."

Chapter 11

The Sled as a Symbol

The red sled in Jonas's first memory from *The Giver* is one of the story's most significant symbols. It is a symbol of the journey that Jonas is embarking upon. It transports him through this new experience of receiving memories, and it also introduces him to other concepts he has never before seen or felt. Hills, snow, and the excitement that Jonas feels during the memory of the ride are all new to him.

The sled also serves as a symbol for the odd mixture of pleasure and pain that memories can hold. As much as Jonas enjoys sliding down the hill on the sled, he also learns about pain. In Chapter 14, he experiences the agonizing pain of a broken leg when the sled tips over. Because of this difficult memory, he begins to understand the pain the Chief Elder spoke about at the ceremony.

The Color Red as a Symbol

Although Jonas cannot see colors at first, the color red becomes a vital symbol in the story. It represents the excitement and passion that Jonas starts to feel when he discovers things he never knew existed. Red is the first color he notices, likely, because it is associated with exhilaration and delight.

Where Does the Color Red Appear in the Novel?

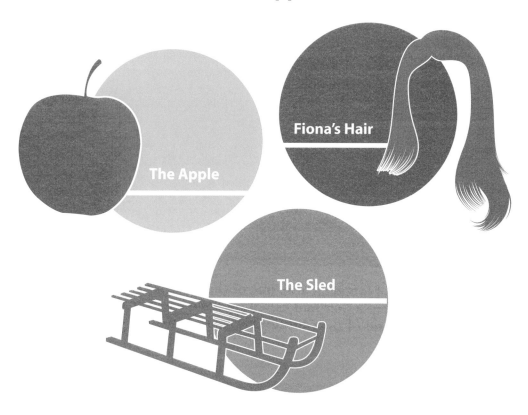

Where Does the Color Red Appear in the Novel?
Assess the author's use of symbolism in the novel.

1. Choose a symbol from the chart and analyze how it appears in the novel. What symbolic significance to the novel does the item have on its own? Why would the author have chosen this item to bear of color? What special meaning does the color imbue on the object?
2. How does this symbol reflect the novel's themes? In a few paragraphs, illustrate the ways in which the author's use of language deepens or weakens the meaning of the color red as a symbol.

Weblink

The Complete Guide to Symbolism
Examine the blog post discussing the usage of symbolism in literature.

1. Contrast and compare examples of analytical descriptions of feelings and sensory descriptions using symbolism from the novel. Which kind is more effective in the novel? Provide reasons for your ideas.
2. Should analytical descriptions play a considerable role in the language of a novel? Why or why not?

Other Symbols in the Novel

The Bicycles

The bicycles, given to all the children in the community when they become Nines, symbolize independence, freedom, maturity, and responsibility.

The Pills

Everyone in the community must start taking a pill each day when they begin to experience Stirrings. With no knowledge or understanding of affection, people in the community are not supposed to fall in love. To the people in the community, the pills are a symbol of adulthood, but in the narrative they are a symbol of suppressed emotions.

The River

A physical boundary, the river that borders the community is a symbol of the limits community members are expected to respect. Later in the book, crossing the river becomes a symbol of leaving the community. Because the first Caleb died in the river, the reader also associates the river with danger.

Writing a Book Review

Students will write a book review of the novel. An exemplary book review will meet the following criteria.

- Grabs the reader's attention with a creative headline
- Begins with an engaging lead to pull the reader into the article
- Introduces the title of the novel, the author, and the genre
- Provides a brief plot description that does not give away the entire story, and makes the reader want to learn more about the novel
- Supports arguments about the novel with accurate and detailed information
- Organizes the review and its arguments in a concise, clear, and logical manner
- Fits the format and style of a book review
- Follows the conventions of print or online journalism
- Demonstrates creativity in their approach
- Writes with a unique, engaging voice and perspective
- Provides fresh insight into the novel
- Provides an honest, authentic opinion on the novel
- Gives a clear recommendation on the novel, backed up by specific textual evidence
- Uses correct spelling, grammar, and punctuation

The Use of Language

Language is a writer's most important tool for telling a story. Some narratives include long, detailed descriptions of both characters and settings, and the language itself may be as beautiful as the places it describes. Other stories use shorter, more exact words and phrases to help the reader visualize people and places within the narratives.

Lowry uses a **journalistic** style in her descriptions of the community and its events at the beginning of *The Giver*. This language is similar to the efficient, succinct style of reporters who write newspaper articles. Lowry focuses on facts, keeping her words and sentences as simple as possible. The precision, efficiency, and sterility of the community is reflected directly by the language of the narrative. This helps readers immerse themselves in Jonas's world more thoroughly.

> "The precision of language was one of the most important tasks of small children. Asher had asked for a smack. The discipline wand, in the hand of the Childcare worker, whistled as it came down across Asher's hands."
>
> Chapter 7

As Jonas begins receiving memories from the Giver, Lowry's language expands. She describes the memories with more expressive words. This lyrical language helps evoke the emotions that Jonas is feeling as he discovers profound concepts such as love and death. She returns to using more straightforward language after Jonas leaves his lessons with the Giver. These changing styles help show the difference between life as it is and how it once was.

> "The sled hit a bump in the hill and Jonas is jarred loose and thrown violently into the air. He fell with his leg twisted under him, and could hear the crack of bone. His face scraped along jagged edges of ice."
>
> Chapter 14

> "Then, the first wave of pain. He gasped. It was as if a hatchet lay lodged in his leg, slicing through each nerve with a hot blade. In his agony, he perceived the word 'fire' and felt flames licking at the torn bone and flesh."
>
> Chapter 14

Euphemisms

Another way Lowry shows the reader how cold and unfeeling people in the community have become is through euphemisms. These are words that mean one thing but sound less harsh. People use euphemisms in the real world every day, often without even realizing it. For example, people might say a person is "on the streets" instead of "homeless," or they might say a person was "let go" instead of "fired."

Lowry's most powerful euphemism in The Giver is the term "release." This word sounds much more humane than "kill." The community members accept that some people must be released because they do not realize what is really happening.

Release

"Needless to say, he will be released, the voice had said, followed by silence. There was an ironic tone to that final message, as if the Speaker found it amusing; and Jonas had smiled a little, though he knew what a grim statement it had been."

Chapter 1

Another euphemism in the story is the term "Nurturer." This term makes it sound like the job involves great caring and support, but the truth is that being a Nurturer requires the person to kill sick or weak community members. Euphemisms soften how the words are perceived, but they do not change their true meanings.

Nurturers

"Jonas's father title was Nurturer. He and the other Nurturers were responsible for all the physical and emotional needs of every newchild during its earliest life. It was a very important job, Jonas knew . . ."

Chapter 1

👁 First Hand

The Rereading Mission, Round 1: *The Giver* by Lois Lowry
Examine the blog post by *Divergent* author Veronica Roth.

1. Roth suggests that one's work does not need to be perfect in order to be powerful. Can you think of examples that prove this statement true? How could a writer's pursuit of perfection hinder a novel?

2. Roth states that *The Giver* taught her that life is valuable even if it is imperfect, and that people should never be discarded. How might one apply this message to their daily lives? Think of real-life examples in the modern world that run counter to this message. How can people combat or prevent this?

🌐 Weblink

7 Quotes That Explain Why *The Giver* Was Such An Important Book To Us When We Were Kids
Examine the blog post discussing Lowry's use of language in *The Giver*.

1. The novel makes a great deal about the burden of choice in life. How important is it to choose a life path for yourself? How might these choices be predetermined for some people?

2. When might the government's removal of certain choices for its citizens be a good thing? Argue your positions with clear reasoning.

Holding a Classroom Debate

Students will form groups and prepare arguments for a debate on a controversial issue. Exemplary performance in a debate will meet the following criteria.

- Demonstrates in-depth understanding of the topic and related information
- Presents strong, logical, and convincing arguments
- Communicates in a clear and confident manner
- Maintains eye contact
- Uses clear vocal tone and a reasonable rate of vocal delivery
- Uses respectful and appropriate language and body language
- Delivers arguments, evidence, and counter-evidence in an engaging and persuasive manner
- Supports each major point of an argument with several relevant and detailed facts and examples
- Connects all arguments to the overall topic in a clear, concise, and organized manner
- Presents the arguments and supporting evidence in a clear, logical manner
- Presents clear, thorough, and accurate information throughout the debate
- Addresses all of the opposing team's arguments with counter-arguments
- Identifies any weakness in the opposing team's arguments
- Constructs strong and relevant counter-arguments using accurate information
- Presents strong and persuasive arguments throughout the debate
- Summarizes the arguments in the closing statement

Impact of the Novel at the Time of Publishing

*T*he *Giver* quickly became Lowry's most successful book. Although many people enjoyed *The Giver*, the book also had its share of critics. Some critics thought the book should not be read in schools or be available in libraries because of its dark subject matter.

The Giver received the Newbery Medal in 1994. In Lowry's acceptance speech, she likened the act of encouraging reading to the work of the Giver. "Each time a child opens a book, he pushes open the gate that separates him from Elsewhere," Lowry said. "The man that I named the Giver passed along to the boy knowledge, history, memories, color, pain, laughter, love, and truth. Every time you place a book in the hands of a child, you do the same thing."

Banned!

Because the subject matter of The Giver is controversial, many people have tried to ban the book from schools. The Giver was the 11th-most requested book to be removed from schools during the 1990s. By the 2000s, The Giver had dropped to the 23rd spot on the list. Supporters of the book see banning it as **censorship**. They insist that the book encourages students to think about important social issues and form their own opinions.

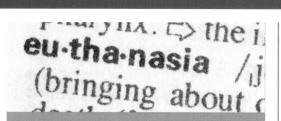

Discussions of Euthanasia and Suicide

The Giver sparked many discussions due to its spotlight on difficult subject matter. The community members in *The Giver* accept the release of members who are old or sick. In real life, the painless killing of an extremely ill person is called **euthanasia**. People have argued for years about whether or not euthanasia is ethical. Suicide is another difficult topic broached by the book. Rosemary essentially kills herself by requesting to be released from the community when she cannot contend with the memories she has received from the Giver.

A Frustrating Ending

The Giver's abrupt and **ambiguous** ending created frustration for some readers. The readers are left to interpret for themselves the result of Jonas's choice. While many readers found this ending unsatisfactory, they seemed to agree that the outcome of Jonas's choice was less important than that he made the decision himself.

The Man on the Cover

The first version of the book's cover includes a black-and-white photograph of an older man with a gray beard. Readers understandably assume him to be the title character. The man in the photograph is actually a famous Swedish painter named Carl Gustaf Nelson, who Lowry took a photo of years earlier while working as a photojournalist.

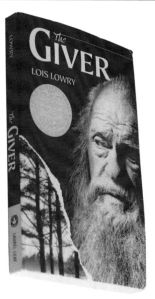

▶ **Video**

**Five Arguments
Against Euthanasia**
Evaluate the arguments against euthanasia presented in the video.

1. Compare and contrast the benefits and dangers inherent in the legalization of euthanasia as an option for the terminally ill. Does assisted dying devalue life? Why or why not?
2. Which argument against euthanasia presented in the video do you think is the strongest? Which argument is the weakest? Provide evidence and reasoning to defend your choices.

🌐 **Weblink**

Why Do So Many Schools Try to Ban *The Giver*?
Examine a blog post from *Slate* discussing the many attempts schools have made to ban *The Giver*.

1. The article states that Texas has tried to ban *The Giver* more times than any other state. What might be the reasons for this? Are these reasons fair?
2. Is it ever ethical or right to ban a book? Imagine a situation in which banning might be justified and explain your reasoning.
3. Are you more or less inclined to read or view materials that have been banned? What might be the reasons for your inclination?

EXTENSION ACTIVITY

Analyzing a Newspaper Article

Students will assess a newspaper article and write an analysis. An exemplary analysis will meet the following criteria.

- Identifies the topic of the article
- Identifies the main points and opinions presented in the article
- Identifies the writer of the article
- Presents information about the writer and infers how his or her life may have shaped this opinion
- Assesses the writer's reliability
- Analyzes how the writer makes his or her argument
- Uses evidence from the article to show how the writer supports his or her argument
- Analyzes the writer's use of literary devices to enhance the article
- Differentiates between the facts and opinions presented in the article
- Identifies when and where the article was published, and determines its intended audience
- Identifies and understands the goals of the article
- Assesses the effectiveness of the format (a newspaper opinion article) in presenting the writer's argument
- Connects the article to the societal and historical context in which it was written
- Infers what is not said about this topic in the article
- Identifies what information is unintentionally implied in the article
- Infers what other opinions may be presented about this topic and who may be most likely to express them
- Uses a number of other resources to analyze the context of the article

Impact of the Novel Now

*T*he *Giver* continues to have an enormous impact on its readers, as well as on the genre of dystopian literature in general. Many young people are hooked yet left wanting more after reading *The Giver*. They want to know what happened after this book's vague ending, and they also look for other books about similarly restrictive societies, which have become increasingly available.

The Giver
has sold more than
12 million copies
since its first publication
in **1993**.

The novel
*has been translated
into more than*
20 different languages
*for readers
across the world*.

The Giver Quartet
has spent a total of
110 weeks on
the *New York Times*
Children's Series Best
Seller List.

The Pioneer of Dystopian Novels

Lowry is often credited with starting the trend of young adult dystopian novels. From *The Hunger Games* to *The Maze Runner*, the number of stories set in dystopian societies has been markedly increasing since Lowry published *The Giver*. Lowry, however, does not categorize her novel as dystopian. "I didn't think of it as futuristic or dystopian or science fiction or fantasy," she told *National Public Radio* in 2014. She sees it as a story about a young person making sense of a complicated world—a theme common to many of her books.

Answering the Questions

After *The Giver*, Lowry wrote *Gathering Blue*, *Messenger*, and *Son*, of which *Son* in particular offers answers about *The Giver's* ending. Today, these four books are sold as a set called *The Giver Quartet*. In 2012, Lowry told *Entertainment Weekly*, "I liked the ambiguity of [*The Giver's*] ending. Over the years, though, it became clear that younger readers in particular did not." Lowry's mailbox was filled with letters from readers curious about Jonas's fate. "I suppose after a period of time, it made me wonder as well," she said.

Film Adaptation

In 2014, film adaptation of *The Giver* was released in theaters, co-written by screenwriters Michael Mitnick and Robert B. Weide. Mitnick was a noted fan of *The Giver*, having first read it when he was in the fifth grade. In an interview with *National Public Radio*, he reveals he completed about 87 drafts of the script.

A Novel About Antiestablishment

The Giver is a book that opens children's eyes to the dangers of conformity. Lowry, who grew up on military bases, says she "was always vaguely at odds with the rigidly ordered lives that [the military] valued and that I was for the most part forced to live." In 1952, when Lowry was 15, she encountered the newly-published *The Catcher in the Rye*, which would become the iconic **antiestablishment** novel for her generation. "*The Giver* has been that for many of today's kids," she says. "[It is] the book that confirms their feeling that the governing body, be it president or parents, may be *getting it wrong*."

▶ Video

Why Socrates Hated Democracy
Analyze the video discussing the frustrations that Greek philosopher Socrates had with democracy.

1. In what way are Socrates's concerns about the failings of democracy evidenced in the failings of the United States government today? What could be done to improve matters?
2. If "democracy is only as good as the education system that surrounds it," what does the United States democracy say about its education system? Explain your ideas.
3. What reasons might the narrator have for saying the United States has "elected many sweet shop owners and very few doctors"?

🌐 Weblink

How Faithful Is *The Giver* to the Lois Lowry Novel?
Assess portions of the *Slate* blog post discussing the 2014 film adaptation of *The Giver's* faithfulness to the novel.

1. When is it appropriate to change aspects of characters or sequences of events during the process of adaptation? When are changes such as these inappropriate?
2. What stands to be lost in the process of adaptation? When can losing elements of the original novel be beneficial? Provide reasons for your opinions.

Creating a Timeline

Students will explore a topic related to the novel and create a timeline to present their research on historical events connected to this topic. An exemplary timeline will meet the following criteria.

- Includes the most significant events pertaining to the topic to be compared and analyzed
- Includes interesting events
- Uses accurate information for all events, including date, location, and major details
- Orders the events in a chronological sequence
- Describes each event with accurate, vivid, and specific details
- Presents the topic from three or more perspectives
- Inspires the reader to ask thoughtful questions regarding the events and perspectives presented in the timeline
- Uses correct spelling, grammar, and punctuation
- Presents the timeline in a visually attractive and striking manner
- Presents the timeline in a neat, organized manner that is logical and easy to follow
- Uses creativity to present the timeline in an engaging manner
- Effectively communicates the historical information relating to the topic
- Supports each event with reliable sources
- Expresses a clear purpose for creating the timeline
- Enhances the reader's understanding of the topic
- Includes a correctly formatted bibliography of all sources used to create the timeline

Perspectives on Freedom of Expression

The danger of conformity is one of the strongest themes in *The Giver*. Lowry depicted this danger to an extreme, showing the reader how horrible the results of blind obedience can be. Her characters cannot make basic choices for themselves, and most of them even stopped thinking for themselves. They had no autonomy whatsoever.

Banning *The Giver* may have helped make it even more popular. In many ways, banning a book makes people more interested in reading the story, but the issue goes deeper than curiosity. Freedom of expression is essential to resisting conformity. It is also part of the foundation of the United States of America.

Timeline of Freedom of Speech

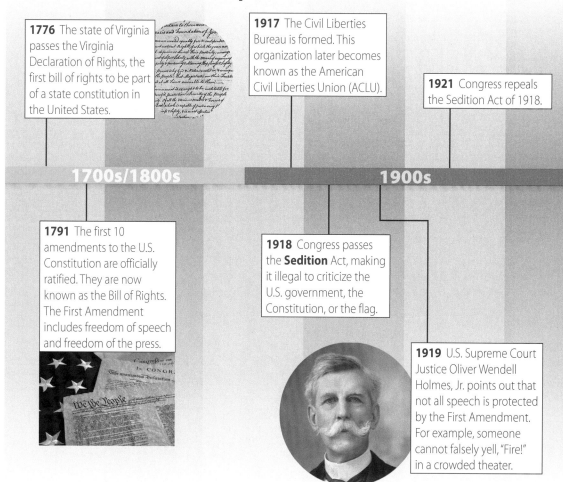

1776 The state of Virginia passes the Virginia Declaration of Rights, the first bill of rights to be part of a state constitution in the United States.

1917 The Civil Liberties Bureau is formed. This organization later becomes known as the American Civil Liberties Union (ACLU).

1921 Congress repeals the Sedition Act of 1918.

1700s/1800s

1900s

1791 The first 10 amendments to the U.S. Constitution are officially ratified. They are now known as the Bill of Rights. The First Amendment includes freedom of speech and freedom of the press.

1918 Congress passes the **Sedition** Act, making it illegal to criticize the U.S. government, the Constitution, or the flag.

1919 U.S. Supreme Court Justice Oliver Wendell Holmes, Jr. points out that not all speech is protected by the First Amendment. For example, someone cannot falsely yell, "Fire!" in a crowded theater.

Soon after the U.S. Constitution was ratified, a list of amendments called the Bill of Rights was added to this governing document. Many Americans consider the First Amendment the most important right. This law prevents the government from restricting a person's right to speak freely or from restricting the press from reporting to the public.

In time, the U.S. Supreme Court interpreted this law to protect more than the freedoms of speech or the press. This right extends to all forms of expression. As the American Civil Liberties Union states, "The First Amendment embodies the belief that in a free and democratic society, individual adults must be free to decide for themselves what to read, write, paint, draw, compose, see, and hear." The law would continue to be challenged through censorship, like book banning, and even through additional legislation, such as the Sedition Act.

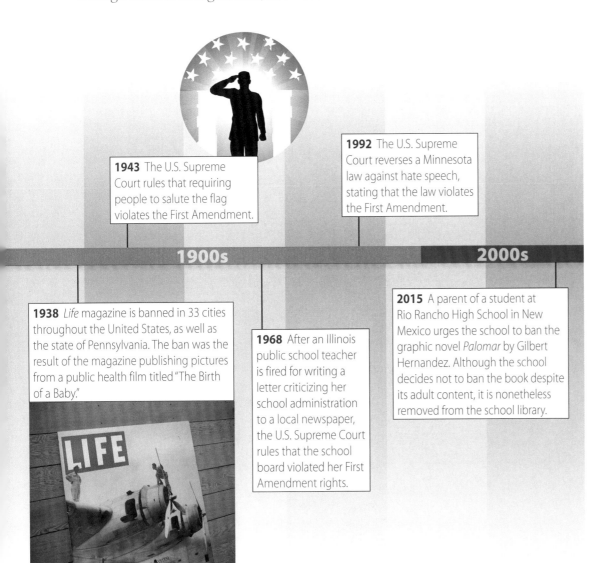

1943 The U.S. Supreme Court rules that requiring people to salute the flag violates the First Amendment.

1992 The U.S. Supreme Court reverses a Minnesota law against hate speech, stating that the law violates the First Amendment.

1900s

2000s

1938 *Life* magazine is banned in 33 cities throughout the United States, as well as the state of Pennsylvania. The ban was the result of the magazine publishing pictures from a public health film titled "The Birth of a Baby."

1968 After an Illinois public school teacher is fired for writing a letter criticizing her school administration to a local newspaper, the U.S. Supreme Court rules that the school board violated her First Amendment rights.

2015 A parent of a student at Rio Rancho High School in New Mexico urges the school to ban the graphic novel *Palomar* by Gilbert Hernandez. Although the school decides not to ban the book despite its adult content, it is nonetheless removed from the school library.

⟳ Transparency– Timeline

Timeline of Freedom of Speech
Examine the historical, cultural, and contemporary contexts shown on the timeline of freedom of speech. Then, contrast and correlate its elements with the themes and events present in *The Giver*.

1. In what ways can historical events, culture, and social mores influence a population's perspective on topics such as freedom of speech? How might these elements shape the way in which a reader interprets the novel? Why is it important to understand the era and context in which a novel is written?

2. How might the era in which Lois Lowry wrote *The Giver* have influenced the novel's themes and settings? Where in the novel is this most evident? Argue your position with clear reasoning.

3. Which current events, changes in laws, new ideas, or political discussions are shaping freedoms of speech in the United States today? On the whole, are freedoms of speech increasing or decreasing in the twenty-first century? Why might this be?

4. How might current events and present perspectives affect the way a reader interprets the topic of freedom of speech as depicted in the novel?

Writing a Comparative Essay

Students will compare two literary devices used in the novel, and then write a comparative essay based on their analysis. An exemplary comparative essay will meet the following criteria.

- Consists of a one-paragraph introduction, three body paragraphs, and a one-paragraph conclusion
- Introduction includes an engaging lead statement about the topic of the essay, more detailed information about the novel, and a one-sentence thesis that specifically states the essay's argument
- Body paragraphs include a topic sentence that refers to the thesis and how the idea appears in the novel, a supporting sentence that points to this part of the novel, textual evidence of this idea from the novel, and analysis of this evidence
- Body paragraphs end with a transition to the next paragraph
- Conclusion refers to the topic of the essay and the three points presented in the body paragraphs, and restates the thesis
- Provides a thorough analysis of the literary devices in question
- Cites strong and thorough textual evidence to support analysis of what the novel says explicitly
- Presents a clear, specific thesis that indicates a high level of critical engagement
- Organizes ideas in a logical manner
- Communicates arguments in a clear, effective manner
- Properly integrates all quotations
- Correctly cites all sources used
- Correctly formats bibliography

Writing a Comparative Essay

*T*he Giver includes some fascinating characters and themes. After reading the novel, write a comparative essay to contrast how two literary devices are used in the narrative. You may compare two characters, themes, symbols, or settings. A comparative essay needs a well-formed argument. You must clearly state both the differences and similarities between the two literary devices you choose to explore. Offer evidence for your position using logical thoughts and quotes from the novel as examples.

How to Analyze and Compare Characters

Use the chart below to guide your comparison between two characters in *The Giver*.

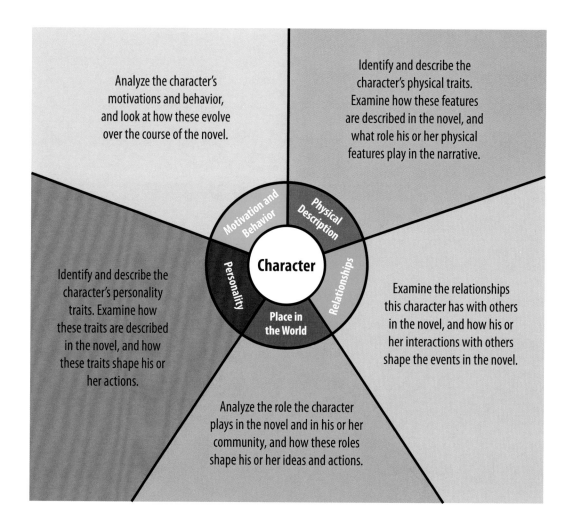

Comparing Jonas and the Giver

Jonas

Personality
- Sensitive and curious
- Polite
- Compassionate
- Quick to conform
- Angry and frustrated after training with the Giver
- Feels deep emotions, such as love

Place in the World
- Protagonist
- Just like everyone else at beginning of story
- Chosen to become the new Receiver of Memory

Motivation and Behavior
- Excited yet anxious about his new job assignment
- Passionate about the things he sees and feels during his training with the Giver
- Feels isolated when he cannot share his knowledge and feelings with family or friends
- Thinks memories should be shared with everyone

Relationships
- Son
- Brother to Lily
- Friend to Fiona and Asher

Physical Description
- Young boy, becoming a Twelve as the story begins
- Pale eyes

The Giver

Place in the World
- Jonas's teacher
- Adviser to community members

Physical Description
- Older man
- Tired-looking
- Long beard and wrinkles
- Pale eyes
- Wears same clothing as the Elders of the community

Motivation and Behavior
- Happy to share pleasant memories with Jonas
- Hesitant to share painful memories with Jonas
- Hopeful that Jonas might change things for the community

Relationships
- Loved Rosemary
- Loves Jonas
- Respected by community members
- Separate from most people

Personality
- Frustrated
- Lonely
- Kind
- Wise

TEACHER NOTES

Transparency– Chart

Questions for Character Analysis

Analyze how specific character features, such as conflicts, motivations, relationships, place in the world, and personality affect the plot of *The Giver*. Cite strong and thorough textual evidence to support your analysis of what the novel says explicitly as well as the inferences you may have drawn from the novel's setting, themes, and symbols.

Quiz Answers
1. C
2. A
3. B
4. D
5. A
6. C
7. C
8. B
9. D
10. A

Key Words

ambiguous: not clear, vague to the point of being confusing

antiestablishment: opposition or hostility towards the social, political, and economic principles of the established authority

censorship: the act of examining literature for the purpose of suppressing or deleting parts considered offensive or morally objectionable

conformity: the act of going along with the crowd in its beliefs or behavior

dystopian: relating to an imagined future society that is unpleasant, inhumane, and fear-inducing for its citizens

euthanasia: the act or practice of mercifully killing or permitting the death of sick or injured people or animals in a painless way to help end suffering

journalistic: a style similar to that of a news reporter

sedition: action or rhetoric encouraging others to rebel against the lawful authority of a state or country

transgression: an act that goes against a rule or law

utopian: relating to an imagined society in which everything is perfect or ideal

Literary Terms

action: everything that occurs in a narrative

antagonist: the person or thing that acts in opposition to the protagonist

characterization: the act of describing a character through the person's appearance and personality

climax: the moment of greatest tension in the story's action

conflict: a struggle between two or more opposing forces, creating a tension that must be resolved

dialogue: the spoken conversations that the characters have with each other

euphemism: an inoffensive word substituted for one that is considered offensive or unpleasant

exposition: the beginning of the story, where the characters and setting are introduced

falling action: the events that take place after the climax, leading up to the end of the story

Freytag's Pyramid: a narrative structure consisting of five elements; this includes exposition, rising action, climax, falling action, and resolution

literary elements: components of every literary work

literary techniques: unique structures of a literary work

lyrical: writing that expresses emotions in an imaginative and beautiful way

metaphor: a symbol used in a story as a literary technique

plot: the specific action that propels a story forward

protagonist: the central character in a piece of fiction who must deal with a conflict and often undergoes some type of change as a result

resolution: the end of the story, when the problems are resolved and the action comes to a conclusion

rhetorical question: a question that is asked not to be answered but to make a point

rising action: the events that create increased drama or tension

simile: a direct comparison using the words "like" or "as"

symbolism: a stylistic device using symbols to represent and intensify concepts and ideas

theme: the underlying topic or main idea of a story

Index

actions 12, 14, 15, 16, 28
American Civil Liberties Union
    (ACLU) 26, 27
antagonist 10
Asher 11, 13, 20, 29

banning 22, 26, 27
Bill of Rights 26, 27
Bridgton, Maine 4, 5

Catcher in the Rye, The 25
characterization 12
characters 5, 7, 9, 10, 12,
    13, 14, 15, 16, 18, 20, 23,
    26, 28
conflict 10, 11, 13, 14, 16

dialogue 12
Divergent 10
dystopian 5, 6, 16, 24

Elsewhere 7, 15, 22
ending 23, 24, 25
euphemism 21
euthanasia 23

film 5, 7, 25, 27
Fiona 13, 19, 29
First Amendment 26, 27
Freytag's pyramid 14

Gathering Blue 25

Hammersberg, Katherine 4
Hammersberg, Robert 4
Hawai'i 4
Holes 10
Hunger Games, The 24

journalist 5, 20, 23

killed 15, 16, 21, 23

Life Magazine 27
Lily 9, 13, 29
*Lion, the Witch and the
    Wardrobe, The* 10
literary devices 14, 15, 28
literary techniques 15, 18
Lowry, Donald 5
Lowry, Lois 4, 5, 6, 7, 8, 9,
    12, 14, 17, 20, 21, 22, 23,
    24, 25, 26

Maze Runner, The 24
memory 5, 9, 11, 12, 15, 16,
    17, 18, 20, 22, 23, 29
Messenger 25
metaphor 15
moral 15

National Public Radio 24, 25
Nelson, Carl Gustaf 23
Newbery Medal 22

Pennsylvania 4, 27
plot 14, 15
point of view 15
protagonist 6, 10, 12, 14, 29

red 18, 19
rhetorical questions 15
Robinson Crusoe 10

simile 15
sold 5, 6, 24
Son 25
suicide 23
Summer to Die, A 5
symbolism 18, 19, 28

themes 16, 17, 18, 24, 26, 28
Tokyo, Japan 7
translated 24

United States 4, 26, 27
U.S. Supreme Court 26, 27

values 16, 17, 25

World War II 4

LIGHTB◆X

⊕ SUPPLEMENTARY RESOURCES

Click on the plus icon ⊕ found in the bottom left corner of each spread to open additional teacher resources.

- Download and print the book's quizzes and activities
- Access curriculum correlations
- Explore additional web applications that enhance the Lightbox experience

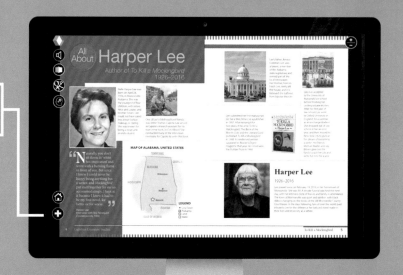

LIGHTBOX DIGITAL TITLES
Packed full of integrated media

VIDEOS

INTERACTIVE MAPS

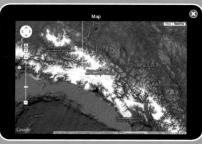

WEBLINKS

SLIDESHOWS

QUIZZES

OPTIMIZED FOR

✓ **TABLETS**

✓ **WHITEBOARDS**

✓ **COMPUTERS**

✓ **AND MUCH MORE!**

Published by Smartbook Media Inc.
350 5th Avenue, 59th Floor New York, NY 10118
Website: www.openlightbox.com

062017
042017

Library of Congress Cataloging-in-Publication Data

Names: Gagne, Tammy author.
Title: The giver / Tammy Gagne.
Description: New York : Smartbook Media Inc., [2018]. |
Series: Lightbox literature studies | Includes index.
Identifiers: LCCN 2016051614 (print) | LCCN 2017006305 (ebook) | ISBN 9781510520158 (hard cover : alk. paper) | ISBN 9781510520165 (multi-user ebk.)
Subjects: LCSH: Lowry, Lois. Giver--Juvenile literature. | Science fiction, American--History and criticism--Juvenile literature.
Classification: LCC PS3562.O923 G5834 2018 (print) | LCC PS3562.O923 (ebook) | DDC 813/.54--dc23
LC record available at https://lccn.loc.gov/2016051614

Printed in Brainerd, Minnesota, United States
1 2 3 4 5 6 7 8 9 0 21 20 19 18 17

Project Coordinator: Jared Siemens
Art Director: Terry Paulhus

Every reasonable effort has been made to trace ownership and to obtain permission to reprint copyright material. The publisher would be pleased to have any errors or omissions brought to its attention so that they may be corrected in subsequent printings. The publisher acknowledges Getty Images, Alamy, and iStock as its primary image suppliers for this title.